2024

JANUARY

WK	M	T	W	T	F	S	S
1	1	2	3	4	5	6	7
2	8	9	10	11	12	13	14
3	15	16	17	18	19	20	21
4	22	23	24	25	26	27	28
5	29	30	31				

FEBRUARY

WK	M	T	W	T	F	S	S
5				1	2	3	4
6	5	6	7	8	9	10	11
7	12	13	14	15	16	17	18
8	19	20	21	22	23	24	25
9	26	27	28	29			

MARCH

WK	M	T	W	T	F	S	S
9					1	2	3
10	4	5	6	7	8	9	10
11	11	12	13	14	15	16	17
12	18	19	20	21	22	23	24
13	25	26	27	28	29	30	31

APRIL

WK	M	T	W	T	F	S	S
14	1	2	3	4	5	6	7
15	8	9	10	11	12	13	14
16	15	16	17	18	19	20	21
17	22	23	24	25	26	27	28
18	29	30					

MAY

WK	M	T	W	T	F	S	S
18			1	2	3	4	5
19	6	7	8	9	10	11	12
20	13	14	15	16	17	18	19
21	20	21	22	23	24	25	26
22	27	28	29	30	31		

JUNE

WK	M	T	W	T	F	S	S
22						1	2
23	3	4	5	6	7	8	9
24	10	11	12	13	14	15	16
25	17	18	19	20	21	22	23
26	24	25	26	27	28	29	30

JULY

WK	M	T	W	T	F	S	S
27	1	2	3	4	5	6	7
28	8	9	10	11	12	13	14
29	15	16	17	18	19	20	21
30	22	23	24	25	26	27	28
31	29	30	31				

AUGUST

WK	M	T	W	T	F	S	S
31				1	2	3	4
32	5	6	7	8	9	10	11
33	12	13	14	15	16	17	18
34	19	20	21	22	23	24	25
35	26	27	28	29	30	31	

SEPTEMBER

WK	M	T	W	T	F	S	S
35							1
36	2	3	4	5	6	7	8
37	9	10	11	12	13	14	15
38	16	17	18	19	20	21	22
39	23	24	25	26	27	28	29
40	30						

OCTOBER

WK	M	T	W	T	F	S	S
40		1	2	3	4	5	6
41	7	8	9	10	11	12	13
42	14	15	16	17	18	19	20
43	21	22	23	24	25	26	27
44	28	29	30	31			

NOVEMBER

WK	M	T	W	T	F	S	S
44					1	2	3
45	4	5	6	7	8	9	10
46	11	12	13	14	15	16	17
47	18	19	20	21	22	23	24
48	25	26	27	28	29	30	

DECEMBER

WK	M	T	W	T	F	S	S
48							1
49	2	3	4	5	6	7	8
50	9	10	11	12	13	14	15
51	16	17	18	19	20	21	22
52	23	24	25	26	27	28	29
1	30	31					

2025

JANUARY

WK	M	T	W	T	F	S	S
1			1	2	3	4	5
2	6	7	8	9	10	11	12
3	13	14	15	16	17	18	19
4	20	21	22	23	24	25	26
5	27	28	29	30	31		

FEBRUARY

WK	M	T	W	T	F	S	S
5						1	2
6	3	4	5	6	7	8	9
7	10	11	12	13	14	15	16
8	17	18	19	20	21	22	23
9	24	25	26	27	28		

MARCH

WK	M	T	W	T	F	S	S
9						1	2
10	3	4	5	6	7	8	9
11	10	11	12	13	14	15	16
12	17	18	19	20	21	22	23
13	24	25	26	27	28	29	30
14	31						

APRIL

WK	M	T	W	T	F	S	S
14		1	2	3	4	5	6
15	7	8	9	10	11	12	13
16	14	15	16	17	18	19	20
17	21	22	23	24	25	26	27
18	28	29	30				

MAY

WK	M	T	W	T	F	S	S
18				1	2	3	4
19	5	6	7	8	9	10	11
20	12	13	14	15	16	17	18
21	19	20	21	22	23	24	25
22	26	27	28	29	30	31	

JUNE

WK	M	T	W	T	F	S	S
22							1
23	2	3	4	5	6	7	8
24	9	10	11	12	13	14	15
25	16	17	18	19	20	21	22
26	23	24	25	26	27	28	29
27	30						

JULY

WK	M	T	W	T	F	S	S
27		1	2	3	4	5	6
28	7	8	9	10	11	12	13
29	14	15	16	17	18	19	20
30	21	22	23	24	25	26	27
31	28	29	30	31			

AUGUST

WK	M	T	W	T	F	S	S
31					1	2	3
32	4	5	6	7	8	9	10
33	11	12	13	14	15	16	17
34	18	19	20	21	22	23	24
35	25	26	27	28	29	30	31

SEPTEMBER

WK	M	T	W	T	F	S	S
36	1	2	3	4	5	6	7
37	8	9	10	11	12	13	14
38	15	16	17	18	19	20	21
39	22	23	24	25	26	27	28
40	29	30					

OCTOBER

WK	M	T	W	T	F	S	S
40		1	2	3	4	5	
41	6	7	8	9	10	11	12
42	13	14	15	16	17	18	19
43	20	21	22	23	24	25	26
44	27	28	29	30	31		

NOVEMBER

WK	M	T	W	T	F	S	S
44						1	2
45	3	4	5	6	7	8	9
46	10	11	12	13	14	15	16
47	17	18	19	20	21	22	23
48	24	25	26	27	28	29	30

DECEMBER

WK	M	T	W	T	F	S	S
49	1	2	3	4	5	6	7
50	8	9	10	11	12	13	14
51	15	16	17	18	19	20	21
52	22	23	24	25	26	27	28
1	29	30	31				

2024 NOTABLE DATES

NEW YEAR'S DAY	JAN 1
NEW YEAR HOLIDAY (SCOTLAND)	JAN 2
CHINESE NEW YEAR (DRAGON)	FEB 10
SHROVE TUESDAY	FEB 13
VALENTINE'S DAY	FEB 14
ST. DAVID'S DAY	MAR 1
INTERNATIONAL WOMEN'S DAY	MAR 8
MOTHER'S DAY (UK) & RAMADAN BEGINS	MAR 10
ST. PATRICK'S DAY	MAR 17
GOOD FRIDAY	MAR 29
EASTER SUNDAY & DAYLIGHT SAVING TIME STARTS	MAR 31
EASTER MONDAY	APR 1
PASSOVER BEGINS	APR 22
ST. GEORGE'S DAY	APR 23
EARLY MAY BANK HOLIDAY	MAY 6
SPRING BANK HOLIDAY	MAY 27
FATHER'S DAY (UK)	JUN 16
ISLAMIC NEW YEAR BEGINS	JUL 6
PUBLIC HOLIDAY (NORTHERN IRELAND)	JUL 12
SUMMER BANK HOLIDAY (SCOTLAND)	AUG 5
SUMMER BANK HOLIDAY (ENG, NIR, WAL)	AUG 26
INTERNATIONAL DAY OF PEACE (UNITED NATIONS)	SEP 21
ROSH HASHANAH (JEWISH NEW YEAR) BEGINS	OCT 2
WORLD MENTAL HEALTH DAY	OCT 10
YOM KIPPUR BEGINS	OCT 11
DAYLIGHT SAVING TIME ENDS	OCT 27
HALLOWEEN	OCT 31
DIWALI	NOV 1
GUY FAWKES NIGHT	NOV 5
REMEMBRANCE SUNDAY	NOV 10
ST. ANDREW'S DAY	NOV 30
CHRISTMAS DAY	DEC 25
BOXING DAY	DEC 26
NEW YEAR'S EVE	DEC 31

PLANNER 2024

JANUARY

1 M
2 T
3 W
4 T
5 F
6 S
7 S
8 M
9 T
10 W
11 T
12 F
13 S
14 S
15 M
16 T
17 W
18 T
19 F
20 S
21 S
22 M
23 T
24 W
25 T
26 F
27 S
28 S
29 M
30 T
31 W

FEBRUARY

1 T
2 F
3 S
4 S
5 M
6 T
7 W
8 T
9 F
10 S
11 S
12 M
13 T
14 W
15 T
16 F
17 S
18 S
19 M
20 T
21 W
22 T
23 F
24 S
25 S
26 M
27 T
28 W
29 T

MARCH

1 F
2 S
3 S
4 M
5 T
6 W
7 T
8 F
9 S
10 S
11 M
12 T
13 W
14 T
15 F
16 S
17 S
18 M
19 T
20 W
21 T
22 F
23 S
24 S
25 M
26 T
27 W
28 T
29 F
30 S
31 S

PLANNER 2024

APRIL

1 M
2 T
3 W
4 T
5 F
6 S
7 S
8 M
9 T
10 W
11 T
12 F
13 S
14 S
15 M
16 T
17 W
18 T
19 F
20 S
21 S
22 M
23 T
24 W
25 T
26 F
27 S
28 S
29 M
30 T

MAY

1 W
2 T
3 F
4 S
5 S
6 M
7 T
8 W
9 T
10 F
11 S
12 S
13 M
14 T
15 W
16 T
17 F
18 S
19 S
20 M
21 T
22 W
23 T
24 F
25 S
26 S
27 M
28 T
29 W
30 T
31 F

JUNE

1 S
2 S
3 M
4 T
5 W
6 T
7 F
8 S
9 S
10 M
11 T
12 W
13 T
14 F
15 S
16 S
17 M
18 T
19 W
20 T
21 F
22 S
23 S
24 M
25 T
26 W
27 T
28 F
29 S
30 S

PLANNER 2024

JULY	AUGUST	SEPTEMBER
1 M	1 T	1 S
2 T	2 F	2 M
3 W	3 S	3 T
4 T	4 S	4 W
5 F	5 M	5 T
6 S	6 T	6 F
7 S	7 W	7 S
8 M	8 T	8 S
9 T	9 F	9 M
10 W	10 S	10 T
11 T	11 S	11 W
12 F	12 M	12 T
13 S	13 T	13 F
14 S	14 W	14 S
15 M	15 T	15 S
16 T	16 F	16 M
17 W	17 S	17 T
18 T	18 S	18 W
19 F	19 M	19 T
20 S	20 T	20 F
21 S	21 W	21 S
22 M	22 T	22 S
23 T	23 F	23 M
24 W	24 S	24 T
25 T	25 S	25 W
26 F	26 M	26 T
27 S	27 T	27 F
28 S	28 W	28 S
29 M	29 T	29 S
30 T	30 F	30 M
31 W	31 S	

PLANNER 2024

OCTOBER

1 T
2 W
3 T
4 F
5 S
6 S
7 M
8 T
9 W
10 T
11 F
12 S
13 S
14 M
15 T
16 W
17 T
18 F
19 S
20 S
21 M
22 T
23 W
24 T
25 F
26 S
27 S
28 M
29 T
30 W
31 T

NOVEMBER

1 F
2 S
3 S
4 M
5 T
6 W
7 T
8 F
9 S
10 S
11 M
12 T
13 W
14 T
15 F
16 S
17 S
18 M
19 T
20 W
21 T
22 F
23 S
24 S
25 M
26 T
27 W
28 T
29 F
30 S

DECEMBER

1 S
2 M
3 T
4 W
5 T
6 F
7 S
8 S
9 M
10 T
11 W
12 T
13 F
14 S
15 M
16 M
17 T
18 W
19 T
20 F
21 S
22 S
23 M
24 T
25 W
26 T
27 F
28 S
29 S
30 M
31 T

JANUARY

GOALS : _____
_____
_____
_____
_____
_____
_____
_____
_____

TO DO : _____
_____
_____
_____
_____
_____
_____
_____

BIRTHDAYS : _____
_____
_____
_____
_____
_____

JANUARY 24

1 MONDAY

NEW YEAR'S DAY

---

2 TUESDAY

NEW YEAR HOLIDAY (SCOTLAND)

---

3 WEDNESDAY

---

4 THURSDAY

FRIDAY 5

SATURDAY 6

SUNDAY 7

NOTES

JANUARY 24

8 MONDAY

9 TUESDAY

10 WEDNESDAY

11 THURSDAY

FRIDAY 12

SATURDAY 13

SUNDAY 14

NOTES

15   MONDAY

16   TUESDAY

17   WEDNESDAY

18   THURSDAY

FRIDAY 19

SATURDAY 20

SUNDAY 21

NOTES

22 MONDAY

---

23 TUESDAY

---

24 WEDNESDAY

---

25 THURSDAY

FRIDAY 26

SATURDAY 27

SUNDAY 28

NOTES

FEBRUARY

GOALS : _____
_____
_____
_____
_____
_____
_____
_____

TO DO : _____
_____
_____
_____
_____
_____

BIRTHDAYS : _____
_____
_____
_____
_____

29   MONDAY

---

30   TUESDAY

---

31   WEDNESDAY

---

1   THURSDAY

FRIDAY 2

F

SATURDAY 3

SUNDAY 4

NOTES

FEBRUARY 24

5   MONDAY

---

6   TUESDAY

---

7   WEDNESDAY

---

8   THURSDAY

FRIDAY   ♥

CHINESE NEW YEAR (DRAGON)

SATURDAY 10

SUNDAY 11

NOTES

FEBRUARY 24

12 MONDAY

---

13 TUESDAY   SHROVE TUESDAY

---

14 WEDNESDAY   VALENTINE'S DAY

---

15 THURSDAY

FRIDAY 16

F

SATURDAY 17

SUNDAY 18

NOTES

19 MONDAY

_____

20 TUESDAY

_____

21 WEDNESDAY

_____

22 THURSDAY

FEBRUARY 24

FRIDAY 23

F

SATURDAY 24

SUNDAY 25

NOTES

T F S S M T W T F S S M T W T F S S M T W T F S S M T W T
1 2 3 4 5 6 7 8 9 10 11 12 13 14 15 16 17 18 19 20 21 22 23 24 25 26 27 28 29

MARCH

GOALS : _____
_____
_____
_____
_____
_____
_____
_____
_____

TO DO : _____
_____
_____
_____
_____
_____

BIRTHDAYS : _____
_____
_____
_____
_____

FEBRUARY 24

WEEK 9

26 MONDAY

27 TUESDAY

28 WEDNESDAY

29 THURSDAY

FRIDAY   1

M

SATURDAY   2

SUNDAY   3

NOTES

4   MONDAY

5   TUESDAY

6   WEDNESDAY

7   THURSDAY

MARCH 24

INTERNATIONAL WOMEN'S DAY

FRIDAY 8

SATURDAY 9

MOTHER'S DAY (UK) & RAMADAN BEGINS

SUNDAY 10

NOTES

11 MONDAY

---

12 TUESDAY

---

13 WEDNESDAY

---

14 THURSDAY

FRIDAY 15

SATURDAY 16

ST. PATRICK'S DAY

SUNDAY 17

NOTES

F S S M T W T F S S M T W T F S S M T W T F S S M T W T F S S
1 2 3 4 5 6 7 8 9 10 11 12 13 14 15 16 17 18 19 20 21 22 23 24 25 26 27 28 29 30 31

18 MONDAY

19 TUESDAY

20 WEDNESDAY

21 THURSDAY

FRIDAY 22

M

SATURDAY 23

SUNDAY 24

NOTES

25 MONDAY

---

26 TUESDAY

---

27 WEDNESDAY

---

28 THURSDAY

GOOD FRIDAY

FRIDAY 29

SATURDAY 30

EASTER SUNDAY & DAYLIGHT SAVING TIME STARTS

SUNDAY 31

NOTES

APRIL

GOALS : _____

_____

_____

_____

_____

_____

_____

TO DO : _____

_____

_____

_____

_____

_____

_____

BIRTHDAYS : _____

_____

_____

_____

_____

_____

APRIL 24

1   MONDAY   EASTER MONDAY

2   TUESDAY

3   WEDNESDAY

4   THURSDAY

FRIDAY   5

SATURDAY   6

SUNDAY   7

NOTES

8 MONDAY

9 TUESDAY

10 WEDNESDAY

11 THURSDAY

FRIDAY   12

_____

SATURDAY   13

_____

SUNDAY   14

_____

NOTES

15 MONDAY

16 TUESDAY

17 WEDNESDAY

18 THURSDAY

FRIDAY 19

SATURDAY 20

SUNDAY 21

NOTES

22 MONDAY   PASSOVER BEGINS

---

23 TUESDAY   ST. GEORGE'S DAY

---

24 WEDNESDAY

---

25 THURSDAY

FRIDAY 26

SATURDAY 27

SUNDAY 28

NOTES

M T W T F S S M T W T F S S M T W T F S S M T W T F S S M T
1 2 3 4 5 6 7 8 9 10 11 12 13 14 15 16 17 18 19 20 21 22 23 24 25 26 27 28 29 30

MAY

GOALS : _____
_____
_____
_____
_____
_____
_____

TO DO : _____
_____
_____
_____
_____
_____
_____

BIRTHDAYS : _____
_____
_____
_____
_____

29 MONDAY

---

30 TUESDAY

---

1 WEDNESDAY

---

2 THURSDAY

FRIDAY   3

_____

SATURDAY   4

_____

SUNDAY   5

_____

NOTES

MAY 24

6   MONDAY   EARLY MAY BANK HOLIDAY

---

7   TUESDAY

---

8   WEDNESDAY

---

9   THURSDAY

FRIDAY 10

SATURDAY 11

M

SUNDAY 12

NOTES

13 MONDAY

14 TUESDAY

15 WEDNESDAY

16 THURSDAY

SATURDAY 18

M

SUNDAY 19

NOTES

20 MONDAY

---

21 TUESDAY

---

22 WEDNESDAY

---

23 THURSDAY

FRIDAY 24

SATURDAY 25

M

SUNDAY 26

NOTES

JUNE

GOALS : _____

_____

_____

_____

_____

_____

_____

_____

TO DO : _____

_____

_____

_____

_____

_____

_____

BIRTHDAYS : _____

_____

_____

_____

_____

27 MONDAY   SPRING BANK HOLIDAY

---

28 TUESDAY

---

29 WEDNESDAY

---

30 THURSDAY

FRIDAY   31

SATURDAY   1

SUNDAY   2

NOTES

3   MONDAY

_____

4   TUESDAY

_____

5   WEDNESDAY

_____

6   THURSDAY

FRIDAY   7

SATURDAY   8

SUNDAY   9

NOTES

10 MONDAY

---

11 TUESDAY

---

12 WEDNESDAY

---

13 THURSDAY

FRIDAY 14

SATURDAY 15

FATHER'S DAY (UK)

SUNDAY 16

NOTES

17 MONDAY

18 TUESDAY

19 WEDNESDAY

20 THURSDAY

JUNE 24

FRIDAY 21

SATURDAY 22

SUNDAY 23

NOTES

24 MONDAY

---

25 TUESDAY

---

26 WEDNESDAY

---

27 THURSDAY

JUNE 24

FRIDAY 28

SATURDAY 29

SUNDAY 30

NOTES

JULY

GOALS : ————————————————————
_____
_____
_____
_____
_____
_____

TO DO : ————————————————————
_____
_____
_____
_____
_____
_____

BIRTHDAYS : ————————————————————
_____
_____
_____
_____
_____

1   MONDAY

2   TUESDAY

3   WEDNESDAY

4   THURSDAY

FRIDAY   5

ISLAMIC NEW YEAR BEGINS   **SATURDAY   6**

SUNDAY   7

NOTES

JULY 24

8   MONDAY

---

9   TUESDAY

---

10   WEDNESDAY

---

11   THURSDAY

JULY 24

FRIDAY 12

SATURDAY 13

SUNDAY 14

NOTES

M T W T F S S M T W T F S S M T W T F S S M T W T F S S M T W
1 2 3 4 5 6 7 8 9 10 11 12 13 14 15 16 17 18 19 20 21 22 23 24 25 26 27 28 29 30 31

15 MONDAY

16 TUESDAY

17 WEDNESDAY

18 THURSDAY

JULY 29

FRIDAY 19

SATURDAY 20

SUNDAY 21

NOTES

M T W T F S S M T W T F S S M T W T F S S M T W T F S S M T W
1 2 3 4 5 6 7 8 9 10 11 12 13 14 15 16 17 18 19 20 21 22 23 24 25 26 27 28 29 30 31

22 MONDAY

23 TUESDAY

24 WEDNESDAY

25 THURSDAY

JULY 24

FRIDAY 26

SATURDAY 27

SUNDAY 28

NOTES

M T W T F S S M T W T F S S M T W T F S S M T W T F S S M T W
1 2 3 4 5 6 7 8 9 10 11 12 13 14 15 16 17 18 19 20 21 22 23 24 25 26 27 28 29 30 31

AUGUST

GOALS : ——————————————————————————

——————————————————————————————————

——————————————————————————————————

——————————————————————————————————

——————————————————————————————————

——————————————————————————————————

——————————————————————————————————

TO DO : ——————————————————————————

——————————————————————————————————

——————————————————————————————————

——————————————————————————————————

——————————————————————————————————

——————————————————————————————————

BIRTHDAYS : ————————————————————————

——————————————————————————————————

——————————————————————————————————

——————————————————————————————————

——————————————————————————————————

——————————————————————————————————

29 MONDAY

30 TUESDAY

31 WEDNESDAY

1 THURSDAY

FRIDAY   2

SATURDAY   3

SUNDAY   4

NOTES

AUGUST 24

5   MONDAY   SUMMER BANK HOLIDAY (SCOTLAND)

---

6   TUESDAY

---

7   WEDNESDAY

---

8   THURSDAY

FRIDAY 9

_____

SATURDAY 10

_____

SUNDAY 11

_____

NOTES

12 MONDAY

---

13 TUESDAY

---

14 WEDNESDAY

---

15 THURSDAY

FRIDAY 16

SATURDAY 17

SUNDAY 18

NOTES

19 **MONDAY**

20 **TUESDAY**

21 **WEDNESDAY**

22 **THURSDAY**

FRIDAY 23

SATURDAY 24

SUNDAY 25

NOTES

SEPTEMBER

GOALS : _____
_____
_____
_____
_____
_____
_____

TO DO : _____
_____
_____
_____
_____
_____

BIRTHDAYS : _____
_____
_____
_____
_____

AUGUST 24

26 MONDAY   SUMMER BANK HOLIDAY (ENG, NIR, WAL)

---

27 TUESDAY

---

28 WEDNESDAY

---

29 THURSDAY

FRIDAY 30

SATURDAY 31

SUNDAY 1

S

NOTES

2 MONDAY

3 TUESDAY

4 WEDNESDAY

5 THURSDAY

FRIDAY   6

SATURDAY   7

SUNDAY   8

S

NOTES

SEPTEMBER 24

♥ **MONDAY**

10 **TUESDAY**

11 **WEDNESDAY**

12 **THURSDAY**

FRIDAY 13

SATURDAY 14

SUNDAY 15

S

NOTES

16   MONDAY

17   TUESDAY

18   WEDNESDAY

19   THURSDAY

FRIDAY 20

INTERNATIONAL DAY OF PEACE (UNITED NATIONS)

SATURDAY 21

SUNDAY 22

NOTES

23 MONDAY

24 TUESDAY

25 WEDNESDAY

26 THURSDAY

FRIDAY 27

SATURDAY 28

SUNDAY 29

S

NOTES

OCTOBER

GOALS : _____
_____
_____
_____
_____
_____
_____
_____
_____
_____

TO DO : _____
_____
_____
_____
_____
_____
_____

BIRTHDAYS : _____
_____
_____
_____
_____

30 MONDAY

---

1 TUESDAY

---

2 WEDNESDAY   ROSH HASHANAH (JEWISH NEW YEAR) BEGINS

---

3 THURSDAY

FRIDAY 4

SATURDAY 5

SUNDAY 6

NOTES

OCTOBER 24

7   MONDAY

---

8   TUESDAY

---

9   WEDNESDAY

---

10   THURSDAY   WORLD MENTAL HEALTH DAY

YOM KIPPUR BEGINS

FRIDAY 11

SATURDAY 12

SUNDAY 13

NOTES

14   MONDAY

15   TUESDAY

16   WEDNESDAY

17   THURSDAY

FRIDAY 18

SATURDAY 19

SUNDAY 20

NOTES

21 MONDAY

---

22 TUESDAY

---

23 WEDNESDAY

---

24 THURSDAY

OCTOBER 24

FRIDAY 25

SATURDAY 26

DAYLIGHT SAVING TIME ENDS

SUNDAY 27

NOTES

T W T F S S M T W T F S S M T W T F S S M T W T F S S M T W T
1 2 3 4 5 6 7 8 9 10 11 12 13 14 15 16 17 18 19 20 21 22 23 24 25 26 27 28 29 30 31

NOVEMBER

GOALS : _____
_____
_____
_____
_____
_____
_____
_____

TO DO : _____
_____
_____
_____
_____
_____

BIRTHDAYS : _____
_____
_____
_____
_____

28 MONDAY

---

29 TUESDAY

---

30 WEDNESDAY

---

31 THURSDAY   HALLOWEEN

NOVEMBER 24

DIWALI

FRIDAY 1

SATURDAY 2

SUNDAY 3

NOTES

4 MONDAY

---

5 TUESDAY GUY FAWKES NIGHT

---

6 WEDNESDAY

---

7 THURSDAY

FRIDAY 8

SATURDAY 9

REMEMBRANCE SUNDAY

SUNDAY 10

NOTES

NOVEMBER 24

11 MONDAY

12 TUESDAY

13 WEDNESDAY

14 THURSDAY

FRIDAY 15

_____

SATURDAY 16

_____

SUNDAY 17

_____

NOTES

18 MONDAY

---

19 TUESDAY

---

20 WEDNESDAY

---

21 THURSDAY

FRIDAY 22

SATURDAY 23

SUNDAY 24

NOTES

F S S M T W T F S S M T W T F S S M T W T F S S M T W T F S
1 2 3 4 5 6 7 8 9 10 11 12 13 14 15 16 17 18 19 20 21 22 23 24 25 26 27 28 29 30

DECEMBER

GOALS : _____

_____

_____

_____

_____

_____

_____

TO DO : _____

_____

_____

_____

_____

BIRTHDAYS : _____

_____

_____

_____

_____

25 MONDAY

26 TUESDAY

27 WEDNESDAY

28 THURSDAY

FRIDAY 29

ST. ANDREW'S DAY

SATURDAY 30

SUNDAY 1

NOTES

DECEMBER 24

WEEK 49

2 MONDAY

---

3 TUESDAY

---

4 WEDNESDAY

---

5 THURSDAY

FRIDAY   6

SATURDAY   7

SUNDAY   8

NOTES

9   MONDAY

10   TUESDAY

11   WEDNESDAY

12   THURSDAY

DECEMBER 24

FRIDAY 13

SATURDAY 14

SUNDAY 15

NOTES

D

DECEMBER 24

16 MONDAY

17 TUESDAY

18 WEDNESDAY

19 THURSDAY

FRIDAY 20

SATURDAY 21

SUNDAY 22

NOTES

DECEMBER 24

23 MONDAY

24 TUESDAY

25 WEDNESDAY   CHRISTMAS DAY

26 THURSDAY   BOXING DAY

DECEMBER 26

FRIDAY 27

SATURDAY 28

SUNDAY 29

NOTES

30 MONDAY

---

31 TUESDAY   NEW YEAR'S EVE

---

1 WEDNESDAY   NEW YEAR'S DAY

---

2 THURSDAY   NEW YEAR HOLIDAY (SCOTLAND)

FRIDAY   3

SATURDAY   4

SUNDAY   5

NOTES

PLANNER 2025

JANUARY	FEBRUARY	MARCH
1 W	1 S	1 S
2 T	2 S	2 S
3 F	3 M	3 M
4 S	4 T	4 T
5 S	5 W	5 W
6 M	6 T	6 T
7 T	7 F	7 F
8 W	8 S	8 S
9 T	9 S	9 S
10 F	10 M	10 M
11 S	11 T	11 T
12 S	12 W	12 W
13 M	13 T	13 T
14 T	14 F	14 F
15 W	15 S	15 S
16 T	16 S	16 S
17 F	17 M	17 M
18 S	18 T	18 T
19 S	19 W	19 W
20 M	20 T	20 T
21 T	21 F	21 F
22 W	22 S	22 S
23 T	23 S	23 S
24 F	24 M	24 M
25 S	25 T	25 T
26 S	26 W	26 W
27 M	27 T	27 T
28 T	28 F	28 F
29 W		29 S
30 T		30 S
31 F		31 M

PLANNER 2025

APRIL

1 T
2 W
3 T
4 F
5 S
6 S
7 M
8 T
9 W
10 T
11 F
12 S
13 S
14 M
15 T
16 W
17 T
18 F
19 S
20 S
21 M
22 T
23 W
24 T
25 F
26 S
27 S
28 M
29 T
30 W

MAY

1 T
2 F
3 S
4 S
5 M
6 T
7 W
8 T
9 F
10 S
11 S
12 M
13 T
14 W
15 T
16 F
17 S
18 S
19 M
20 T
21 W
22 T
23 F
24 S
25 S
26 M
27 T
28 W
29 T
30 F
31 S

JUNE

1 S
2 M
3 T
4 W
5 T
6 F
7 S
8 S
9 M
10 T
11 W
12 T
13 F
14 S
15 S
16 M
17 T
18 W
19 T
20 F
21 S
22 S
23 M
24 T
25 W
26 T
27 F
28 S
29 S
30 M

PLANNER 2025

JULY	AUGUST	SEPTEMBER
1 T	1 F	1 M
2 W	2 S	2 T
3 T	3 S	3 W
4 F	4 M	4 T
5 S	5 T	5 F
6 S	6 W	6 S
7 M	7 T	7 S
8 T	8 F	8 M
9 W	9 S	9 T
10 T	10 S	10 W
11 F	11 M	11 T
12 S	12 T	12 F
13 S	13 W	13 S
14 M	14 T	14 S
15 T	15 F	15 M
16 W	16 S	16 T
17 T	17 S	17 W
18 F	18 M	18 T
19 S	19 T	19 F
20 S	20 W	20 S
21 M	21 T	21 S
22 T	22 F	22 M
23 W	23 S	23 T
24 T	24 S	24 W
25 F	25 M	25 T
26 S	26 T	26 F
27 S	27 W	27 S
28 M	28 T	28 S
29 T	29 F	29 M
30 W	30 S	30 T
31 T	31 S	

PLANNER 2025

OCTOBER

1 W
2 T
3 F
4 S
5 S
6 M
7 T
8 W
9 T
10 F
11 S
12 S
13 M
14 T
15 W
16 T
17 F
18 S
19 S
20 M
21 T
22 W
23 T
24 F
25 S
26 S
27 M
28 T
29 W
30 T
31 F

NOVEMBER

1 S
2 S
3 M
4 T
5 W
6 T
7 F
8 S
9 S
10 M
11 T
12 W
13 T
14 F
15 S
16 S
17 M
18 T
19 W
20 T
21 F
22 S
23 S
24 M
25 T
26 W
27 T
28 F
29 S
30 S

DECEMBER

1 M
2 T
3 W
4 T
5 F
6 S
7 S
8 M
9 T
10 W
11 T
12 F
13 S
14 S
15 M
16 T
17 W
18 T
19 F
20 S
21 S
22 M
23 T
24 W
25 T
26 F
27 S
28 S
29 M
30 T
31 W

ADDRESS / PHONE NUMBERS

NAME

ADDRESS

TELEPHONE   MOBILE

EMAIL

NAME

ADDRESS

TELEPHONE   MOBILE

EMAIL

NAME

ADDRESS

TELEPHONE   MOBILE

EMAIL

NAME

ADDRESS

TELEPHONE   MOBILE

EMAIL

NAME

ADDRESS

TELEPHONE   MOBILE

EMAIL

NAME

ADDRESS

TELEPHONE   MOBILE

EMAIL

ADDRESS / PHONE NUMBERS

NAME

ADDRESS

TELEPHONE   MOBILE

EMAIL

NAME

ADDRESS

TELEPHONE   MOBILE

EMAIL

NAME

ADDRESS

TELEPHONE   MOBILE

EMAIL

NAME

ADDRESS

TELEPHONE   MOBILE

EMAIL

NAME

ADDRESS

TELEPHONE   MOBILE

EMAIL

NAME

ADDRESS

TELEPHONE   MOBILE

EMAIL

NAME

ADDRESS

TELEPHONE   MOBILE

EMAIL

NOTES

NOTES